PUBLISHED BY
THE SUMMIT GROUP
1227 WEST MAGNOLIA
FORT WORTH, TEXAS 76104

Library of Congress Cataloging in
Publication Data

In search of Elvis: a fact filled seek
and find adventure / Summit Group;
edited by Hal A. Brown.
p. cm.
ISBN 1-56530-003-3

1. Presley, Elvis, 1935-1977.
2. Rock musicians—United States
—Humor. I. Brown, Hal A.
II. Summit Group.
ML420.P96I5 1992
784'.0924   QBI92-400

Special thanks to Kyle Mize and
Mark Bezos for contributions
throughout the project and for a
last-minute midnight run to
Memphis.

All illustrations and any references
to those illustrations are fiction,
and any resemblance therein to
actual persons or places is purely
accidental and coincidental.

Printed in Verona, Italy
First Edition

IN SEARCH OF ELVIS

A Fact-Filled Seek-And-Find Adventure

Rick Sales, Illustrator

Leslie Senevey, Copy Writer

Rishi Seth, Designer

ELVIS ATE THE

Okay. When you think of donuts what comes to mind? Coffee, policemen, holes in the middle, Elvis? So maybe Elvis doesn't spring immediately to mind, but his die-hard fans know he had a penchant for donuts. And everyone knows of his sweet tooth in general. While most people purchase donuts by the dozen, Elvis would order them by the hundreds, presumably so he could share with his entourage/extended family, of course. In Memphis, the King's bakery of choice was Radefeld's Bakery, opened in 1957 and now located (appropriately) on Elvis Presley Boulevard. Dean Radefeld still runs the place and has many vivid recollections of the King, his crew, and their donut-dining habits. As with most of Elvis' public outings, his donut shopping sprees took place secretly, after hours, and most often were specially arranged in advance. If a private bakery visit was not possible, or if Elvis' sweet tooth needed instant gratification, he would often send his mother and father or members of his entourage to Radefeld's for donut duty. All you Elvis trivia buffs, take note. His favorite donuts were jelly donuts, and Radefeld's was always sure to have plenty made fresh, just in case one of the King's special orders came in. It's a well-known fact that Elvis' eating habits were the perfect example of "how not to eat," but who's going to tell the King, "No Elvis. You can't have your donuts or your dessert until you eat your vegetables. And while you're at it, you could use a few laps around the block." His mother might have gotten away with this "motherly" command, but she was of the same down-home, country-cooking, everything-with-gravy-on-the-side and extra grease school-of-thought as Elvis. In addition to his regular orders for jelly donuts and the works, Elvis often ordered birthday cakes from Radefeld's and other bakeries (whether it was anyone's birthday or not). His favorite birthday cake designs included guitar-shaped cakes and layer cakes with his picture on top. (He never claimed to be modest.) Although Radefeld's claim to fame is that Elvis ate the whole thing here, Dean Radefeld remains disappointed that he didn't get to bake Elvis's wedding cake. (Since the Presleys were married in Las Vegas, they used caterers there.) Who knows though – maybe Radefeld will still someday get his chance. Elvis has been reportedly sighted at several donut hot spots as of late, and is said to still harbor an obvious passion for jelly donuts. You might find the King at Sal's Donut Factory in Mississippi. Word is, he even picks up a shift from time to time, perhaps out of boredom. Now see if you can find him. Ready, set, dough!

Donut manufacturer introduces its new line of 2.4 lb. Elvis Eclairs

MENDENHALL, MISS. — One of the country's largest producers of donuts, Sal's Donuts, based locally, announced a press conference today the introduction of the Elvis Eclair. Sal's, a well-known breakfast stop of the King's, added the Eclair to its national line because "frankly we were making so many of the special order 2.4 lb. eclairs for Elvis that we

IN A LEAGUE

Among other recreational activities, Elvis enjoyed bowling in his spare time. Anyway, the King was known to rent out a Memphis bowling alley called Bowl Haven Lanes from time to time for his own private "bowl games." No word on whether Elvis was any good at the sport, but it's a safe bet to say that any game that involved recklessly hurling a heavy object across a room was right up Elvis' alley. And the fact that bowling is just about the only game where it's common to see blue suede shoes probably didn't dampen Elvis' liking for the sport. Bill Blackburn, who served as secretary of the Memphis Bowling Association during Elvis' bowling days, claims that if the King's interest in the sport had been more widely known, it would have brought the Memphis Bowling Association more recognition than it had encountered in all its years of existence. Apparently, once word spread that Elvis was a bowling man; bowling temporarily, at least, became the sport of choice in Memphis. Most folks, though, couldn't afford to rent out the entire Bowl

Haven Lanes like Elvis did. Larry Weber, an avid bowler at Bowl Haven during Elvis' bowling period (and who is now the manager of the Brunswick Winchester Bowling Lanes) said that Elvis and his entourage were pretty well-behaved during their "bowl-o-ramas." Although against Bowl Haven policy, they rarely turned in their score sheets. No matter, for the King went down in history anyway for being in a league of his own. Another little known Elvis tidbit: During the 1960s, when Elvis was King of the Screen as well as the King of Rock-and-Roll, he kept several homes in the Hollywood Hills. One of the houses he rented in 1963 in posh Bel Air came complete with a bowling alley in the basement – no doubt one of the drawing points that made the house so appealing to Elvis. These days, it is not uncommon to hear of Elvis hanging out around the gutters of bowling alleys across the country. Time for you to strike out in search of the King. Choose your shoes, let 'er rip, and when the dust has settled, see how many are left standing.

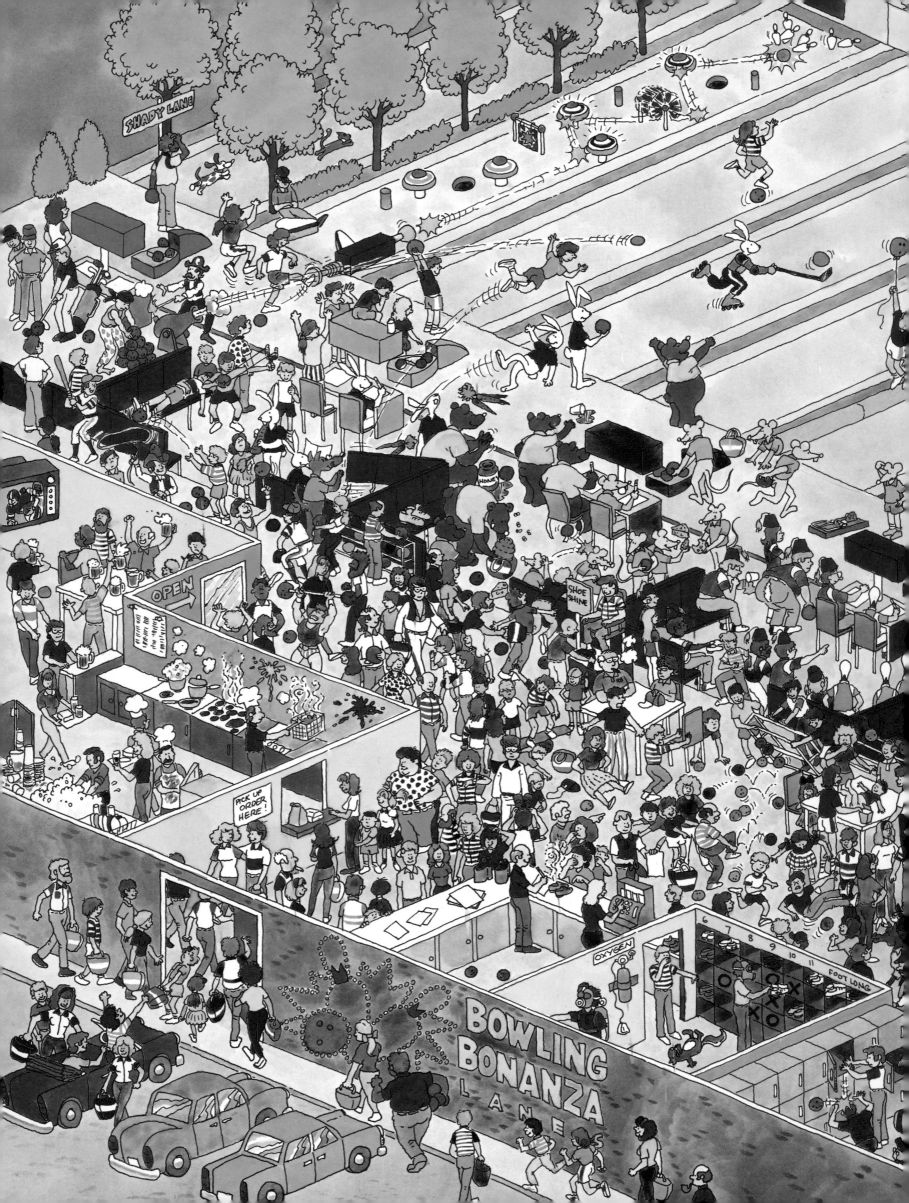

ELVIS TAKE

If Elvis' life were a football game, he could be disqualified for taking the longest time out in history. Maybe dead, maybe not, since 1977, his legend lives on on the football field. Supposedly, as a teenager, Elvis had aspirations to be a letterman on his high school team. He went out for the L.C. Humes High School team in 1951, but unfortunately he never made the cut, so his youthful days of athletic glory were not to be. It seems, however, that Elvis never lost his love for the sport, even as an adult. During his Hollywood days he formed a touch football team of his own, called the Elvis Presley Enterprisers. The Enterprisers played against other Hollywood stars' teams on most weekends. Elvis' passion for television entertainment extended to football: at Graceland, Elvis mounted three television sets in the TV room wall, the better to keep an eye on several football games at once. Atlanta Falcons Head Coach Jerry Glanville (formerly head coach of the Houston Oilers) steadfastly maintains that Elvis is alive and well and still a loyal football fan. Glanville even claims Elvis played in the Houston/ New England Liberty Bowl game. The NFL play-by-play sheet read: "Carlson pass incomplete;

intended receiver Elvis Presley." Since 1988, Glanville has dutifully left two tickets at the will-call window for all of his teams' games. Glanville reports the public's reaction the first time he announced his Elvis idea. "My phone started ringing off the hook – people were spotting Elvis everywhere. Elvis was calling local radio stations; Elvis was eating chicken in the park; Elvis was a doorman at the Peabody [a famous Memphis hotel]; Elvis was leaving messages at my hotel." Supposedly, Glanville's idea to bring Elvis out of hiding (or his eternal time out) worked. The King has reportedly been spotted at dozens of professional football games, most notably at Oilers games. Glanville personally reports spotting the King. "I've personally seen him twice, wearing a leather jacket and sunglasses," he says. "And I get letters every month from Elvis, congratulating me on victories, complimenting my outfits. All the letters, by the way, are postmarked Pasadena, Texas." So keep your eyes peeled, and you may find the King at a playoff game in Atlanta. It's your turn to try to score. Think of it as fourth down with no timeouts left. Turn the page, take the snap, and go for it!

"Gimme an E!"

Elvis makes surprise appearance at playoff game

ATLANTA, GA. – Sixty-five thousand fans were in the presence of royalty Sunday when the King of Rock and Roll took in the playoff contest between Atlanta and Washington. "I can't believe it! I sat next to Elvis Presley," gushed Atlanta native Eddie Ponczek, 42. "I thought he was dead." Presley, who made a quick getaway following the fourth quarter finale, reportedly claimed a ticket left for him

HIS MAJES

Tennis wasn't as brutal as most of the sports Elvis enjoyed, but he was game for just about any game that had to do with love. Although Elvis was not an avid participant in the game of tennis, he was known to be an occasional spectator of the sport. As far as what Elvis and the game of tennis have in common . . . . Well, let's see. Elvis probably admired the wardrobes of the professional tennis players he was rumored to have followed. Their outfits were mostly white, and white, after all, was the color of choice for most of the King's custom-designed costumes. Another similarity between the game of tennis and Elvis can be traced to Graceland itself. Just think of this massive white plantation-style home as Graceland Country Club – the perfect setting for a dignified tennis match. And while Graceland wasn't actually home to a tennis court, it did house an indoor racquetball court, complete with all the amenities to be found at the poshest of private clubs. The private racquetball court was built supposedly so that Elvis wouldn't have to worry about secretly renting public courts after hours (although in 1976 Elvis, his doctor, manager and a real estate developer did invest in a public racquetball court in Memphis that bore his name: the Presley Center Courts). Many a

ELVIS' COURT

hardcore racquetball match was staged at Graceland for Elvis and his buddies. Just think of Elvis' buddies as the country club members. They had to be screened and selected for membership to the private club, and once in, they had to play by the King of the Club's rules. Or else. The backyard building at Graceland that housed the court was also home to a sauna, jacuzzi and fully-equipped weight room. It also held a recreational room with pinball machines, a piano and a jogging track on the roof. Talk about a man's home being his castle. There's still a bit of mystery in connection with the King's court. This was one of the last places he was seen alive before his death in 1977. Spotting him after his death is another story. As a matter of fact, he's been sighted at more tennis tournaments since he died than when he was alive — probably because when he was alive (the first time) he liked to keep a low profile. (Got that? The King's not keeping as low a profile as he did in the old days.) He might now even be spotted on any given day at any tennis tournament in the land. Maybe even at the one on the next page. The ball's in your court now. Try to spot the King. It's your serve.

Elvis seen courtside at tennis tournament finals

POUGHKEEPSIE, NY. — The King of Rock-and-Roll gave new meaning to the term "holding court" yesterday when word swept through the crowd at the East Poughkeepsie Indoor Men's Classic that Elvis Presley was in attendance. Rather inconspicuous in a golf cap, tinted sunglasses, and a sequined jumpsuit, Presley remained silent in his courtside seat.

ELVIS GO

If Elvis were a city, he'd no doubt be Las Vegas. The King possessed a well-known wild streak (like the city); he was flashy and loud (like the city), and he was a definite creature of the night (you guessed it – like the city). The bright lights of Vegas held a special attraction for Elvis. No surprise then, that he was drawn to the neon oasis in the desert like a moth to a 70-watt front porch light bulb. The King worked, played and even got married in Las Vegas. Ironically, the city that could now be called the capital of Elvis impersonators  originally rejected the King's bold brand of rock-and-roll. It was in 1956 that Elvis made his first Las Vegas appearance at the New Frontier Hotel. He was paid $17,500 per week (a pittance compared to his later salaries), billed as the "Atomic-Powered Singer," and did the opening act for comedian Shecky Green in the Venus Room. Unfortunately, the Vegas audience wasn't quite ready for an "atomic-powered" show, and Elvis bombed. Despite this less than spectacular Vegas debut, Elvis would later hit the jackpot and prove to be the master of the Vegas stage show. In 1963, Elvis and the town he grew to love went down in celluloid history, thanks to the film *Viva Las*

ES GOLD

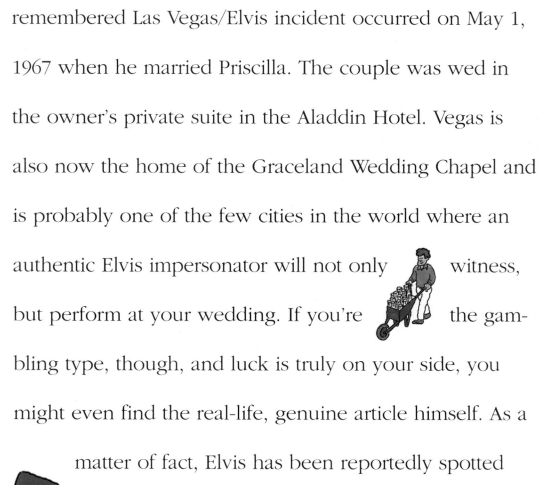

Vegas. The film was shot at various locations around Las Vegas including the University of Nevada, the Flamingo and the Tropicana; but the place where the King most indelibly made his mark was the Sahara Hotel, specifically the Presidential Suite where he and his buddies took up the entire top floor. Elvis continued to play Vegas in the later years of his career, most notably at the Showroom Internationale in 1969. But the single most remembered Las Vegas/Elvis incident occurred on May 1, 1967 when he married Priscilla. The couple was wed in the owner's private suite in the Aladdin Hotel. Vegas is also now the home of the Graceland Wedding Chapel and is probably one of the few cities in the world where an authentic Elvis impersonator will not only witness, but perform at your wedding. If you're the gambling type, though, and luck is truly on your side, you might even find the real-life, genuine article himself. As a matter of fact, Elvis has been reportedly spotted in Vegas since his alleged death in 1977. Now it's your turn to wager. It's a full house at the Casino, and Elvis is on the loose. Place your bets, wish for luck, and see if you can hit the jackpot.

Elvis marries nightclub waitress in Las Vegas

LAS VEGAS, NEV. — According to the Reverend Gary Engelbrecht, owner of The Church of Eternal Love, Elvis and Candy Clampitt were married at 4 a.m. yesterday after Elvis performed at an Elvis impersonator contest at The Star Dust. "Elvis told me he has performed at over 600 impersonation contests since his alleged death in 1977 and never won," Engelbrecht said. "However, he said he came closest at the 1988 Summer

ALOHA AGAI

Girls, fun in the sun, girls, the King of Island Swing Don Ho and girls –what more could a rock-and-roller like Elvis ask for? (Just kidding about Don Ho.) The blue waters of Hawaii, along with the previously mentioned girls, beckoned to Elvis' sense of adventure. Although he never ventured outside the United States (with the exception of his army travels), he often crossed the mainland to catch a wave for his Hawaiian treks. While the islands of Hawaii are most often associated with sprawling on the sand like a beached whale just for the fun of it, Elvis – the hardest working man in rock-and-roll – journeyed to Hawaii for business as much as for pleasure. Hawaii was the site of a legendary Elvis concert in 1961. It was a benefit concert for the *USS Arizona* Memorial, and it was said to be one of the King's most electrifying performances ever. The *Arizona* was one of the American battleships sunk by the Japanese at Pearl Harbor, and Elvis' concert raised $65,000 for its memorial. This benefit concert was also by far the longest ever performed by Elvis, and he supposedly slept for 24 hours straight afterwards. As a matter of fact, the concert apparently gave Elvis a severe case of burnout (not the kind that has anything to do with sunscreen), and he refrained from performing live for the next eight years. In 1973, Elvis once again made history when he broadcast his television special *Elvis: Aloha from Hawaii* from the Honolulu International Center Arena. It was beamed around the world via satellite and it meant that Elvis "went global" before "going global" was "in." In addition to his television special, Elvis made several movies on location in Hawaii including *Paradise Hawaiian Style, Blue Hawaii,* and *Girls! Girls! Girls!* Of course, Elvis' Hawaiian success meant booming business for some of the businesses on the island. Hawaii is now home to one of the only all-Elvis stores outside of Memphis. It's called Elvis, Elvis, Elvis (catchy, huh?) and is located in the King's favorite Hawaii hotel – the Hilton Hawaiian Village in Honolulu, where Elvis stayed for his very first Hawaiian concert in 1957, his epic 1961 benefit concert, his 1973 *Aloha* special, and his last tropical vacation in 1977. Well, surf's up. Take a deep breath, hold your nose, and dive in. See if you can spot the King. And one warning: He's slippery when wet. Aloha.

The King is alive and living in Hawaii

HONOLULU, HAWAII — That's the word from an Indiana housewife who recognized Elvis Presley on the beach while she was here on vacation. "He said he's been living here in Hawaii for the past 14 years," claimed Terry Pruitt of Bloomington, Indiana. According to Mrs. Pruitt, Elvis faked his death not to avoid his fans but instead to "catch some waves and work on his tan," things difficult to manage (see 'Elvis' on page 6)

THE KAR

With Elvis' revolutionary brand of hip-twisting, body-wiggling dance moves, (remember – this was before the days of MTV) it's not surprising to know that he had an intense need to burn up energy and let off steam in other physical pursuits. This was also before the terms "Go for the burn," "cross-training" and "Just do it" had jogged into the American vocabulary. Nevertheless, Elvis was a fitness buff before there really was such a thing, even if he didn't always look it. Karate-kicking was how Elvis got his kicks, and after 20 years of studying the Oriental art, he was practically a master. Elvis was first introduced to the sport during his stint in the army, and he was immediately hooked. Karate gave him a power of movement and control he had never known, if not the agility and flexibility that became some of his most notable on-stage characteristics. Elvis studied karate with several masters, first with Red West of the Tennessee Karate Institute in Memphis, and later with private instructors in his own home. But the King's primary teacher was Kang Rhee, owner of the Kang Rhee Institute of Self-Defense.

Under the tutelage of Rhee, Elvis became a prized pupil and earned several advanced black belts. Elvis once said, "Karate is a way of life. It's so much more than a sport." It's no surprise, then, to know he broke a bone in his hand while performing his own karate stunt scene in the movie *G.I. Blues*. A funny anecdote: Elvis apparently liked his black belts tight and his ghis (karate suits) tighter. He had them specially made by his Las Vegas costume designer so they would fit much like his stage jumpsuits. Unfortunately, they were not made to take a licking and keep on kicking, because the first time Elvis went for a kick, the pants ripped open. Elvis' love of the sport never waned. He often showed off his karate moves in the hallways of Graceland for anyone who would watch. In the early '70s, he even got his wife Priscilla interested in the sport. Is it any wonder, then, that the King has often been spotted at karate events since then? Now it's your turn to see if you can chop the King down to size. Try to spot him at the World Karate Championships – Hiiii Yaaa!

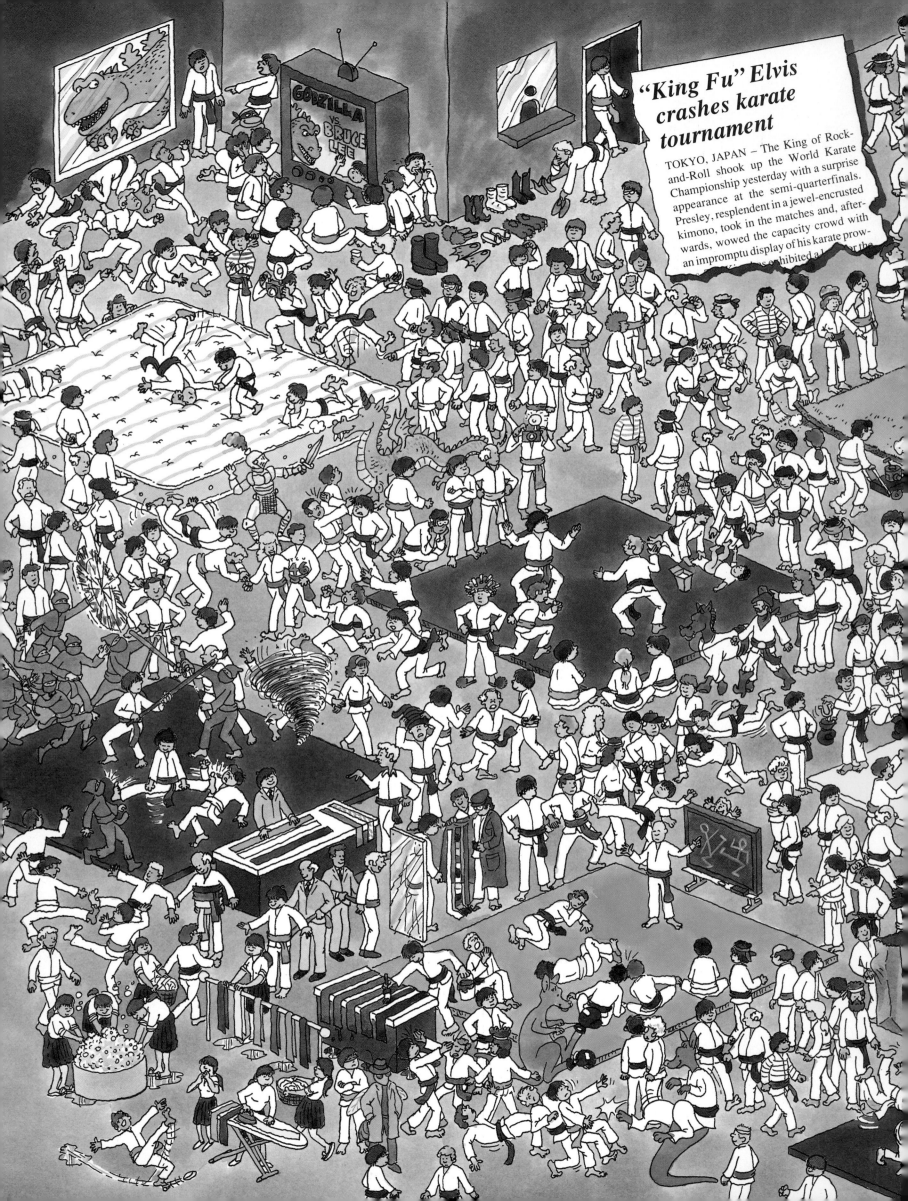

"King Fu" Elvis crashes karate tournament

TOKYO, JAPAN – The King of Rock-and-Roll shook up the World Karate Championship yesterday with a surprise appearance at the semi-quarterfinals. Presley, resplendent in a jewel-encrusted kimono, took in the matches and, afterwards, wowed the capacity crowd with an impromptu display of his karate prow-

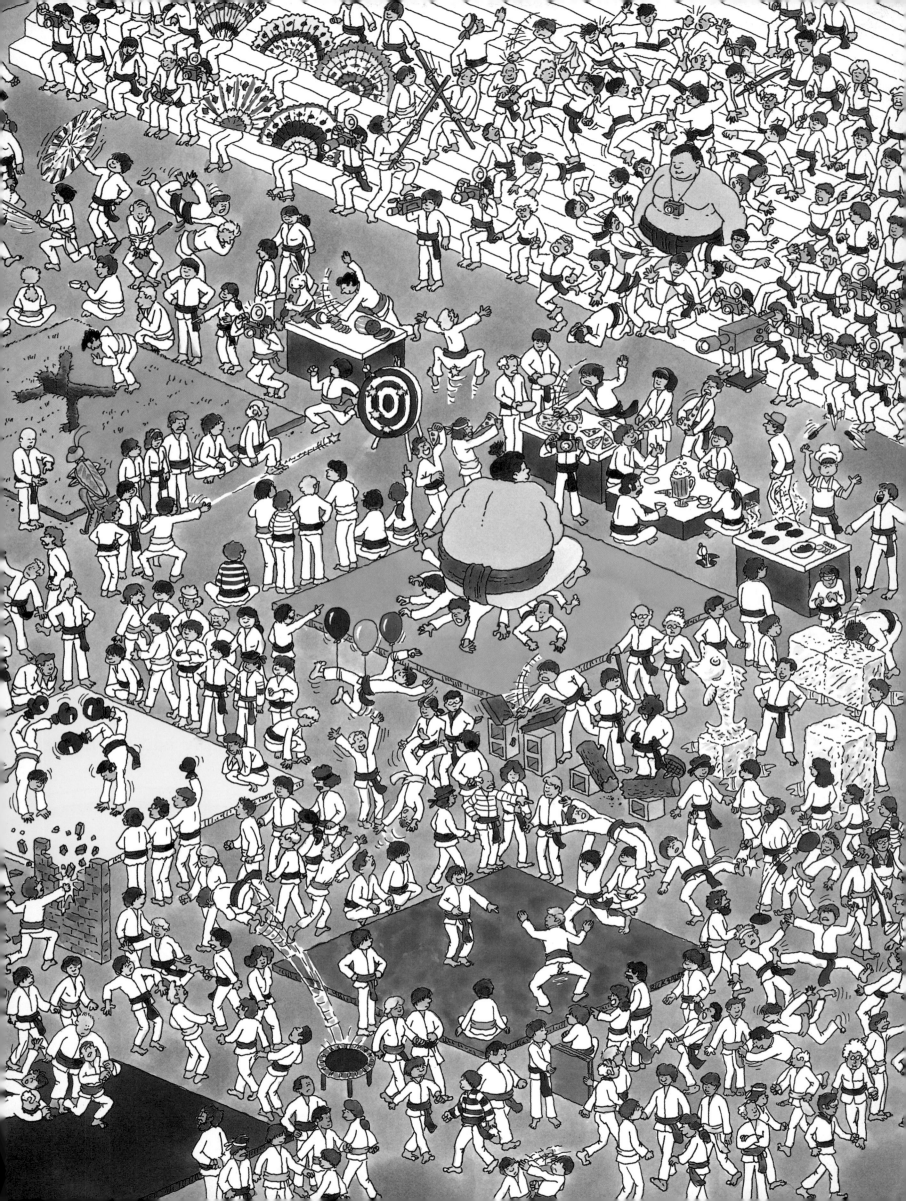

THE UPS & DOWN

When you're the King of Rock-and-Roll (or the king of anything for that matter), the world is at your disposal as far as fun and games go. So what does a king do for fun? If you're Elvis, you rent out an entire amusement park for your own private party. As a small boy, Elvis had snuck into the Fairgrounds to avoid paying the admission fee. What small-town boy wouldn't dream of someday controlling an entire amusement park? In the earlier days of his career, Elvis rented out the Fairgrounds Amusement Park for $2,500 per night (a bargain compared to what it would probably cost today). One of the reasons Elvis rented out the entire park was so that he could avoid being mobbed by crowds of adoring fans. But the other reason (and possibly the primary one) was so that he could personally control the rides. One of his favorite rides was the Pipin Roller Coaster, and he would often take it for 20 spins without stopping. While this type of maniac roller coaster riding was Elvis' idea of fun, other members of his entourage, including Priscilla, simply had to endure the activity and hope not to get sick. Talk about the ups and downs of hanging out with the King. Another of Elvis' favorite amusement park activities (and another activity that could prove harmful to his friends' health) was a rough-and-tumble, bang-'em-up version of the bumper cars. Elvis would split his entire entourage into two teams and stage a sort of bumper cars combat game. The object of the ever-so-dignified game was to ram-slam-jam your car as hard as you could into someone else's (all in the name of good fun, of course). The Fairgrounds Amusement Park is still in operation in Memphis, but it's now called Libertyland. Libertyland, to this day, stages its annual Elvis memorial, which usually takes the form of a "special guest" Elvis impersonator contest during International Tribute Week (held annually in Memphis in remembrance of the King). Some people say that Elvis continues his tradition of secretly renting out Libertyland. And others say they've spotted the King at other amusement parks around the country. See for yourself if you can spot the King at WackoWorld. Admission is free – just turn the page. And have fun.

Elvis photographed at amusement park

ORLANDO, FL. — The King loves the rides, but the real reason he returns to WackoWorld Amusement Park once every year is for the rock candy. That's the word from Ft. Lauderdale, Florida resident Bunny Green, who photographed the singer while visiting the park yesterday with her 12 children. Mrs. Green, 36, said she spotted Presley outside the Tunnel of Love and actually spent all of her kids' ride money to purchase a camera at a gift

Elvis was always one to appreciate a good cheeseburger (well-done, please, and hold the onion). The Gridiron Restaurant, located less than a mile away from Graceland itself, was one of his favorite hangouts. There the burgers were thick and the crowds were thicker, thanks to Elvis and his tight-knit entourage. This old Elvis stomping ground is still around and still grilling 'em up hot and juicy at 4101 Elvis Presley Boulevard. Another of Elvis' favorite hamburger haunts was the Coffee Cup Diner in West Memphis, Arkansas. In the late '50s, the Coffee Cup, no longer in business, was a frequent stopping point for Elvis and his fellow recruits in route to Fort Chaffee. Elvis' taste for the good ol' American burger was a well-known fact as far back as his first post-military recording session. The story goes that Elvis and his gang were secretly cutting an album at the RCA Nashville studio. The project was taking place "underground," so to speak, to avoid the mobs of fans who surfaced anytime Elvis showed up. According to session producer Chet Atkins, Elvis went undetected until the King's appetite for the

OR A KING

Great American Burger kicked in. It was about that time that the Crystal Hamburger Stand near the RCA studio got a call-in order for 100 burgers to go. To go where? Right down the road to the RCA studio, of course. The word spread like a grease fire in the kitchen of a greasy spoon. Elvis was back in town and recording at RCA! So much for secrecy and a burger on the sly. In his later years, hamburgers and other junk food came to be one of the King's major weaknesses. He was labeled a "junk food junkie" by his personal physician, Dr. George Nichopoulos. In fact, Elvis practically had his own private burger joint in the form of the Graceland kitchen staff and servants. Graceland, however, no doubt lacked the gritty down-home ambience of places like the Gridiron, the Coffee Cup, and the Crystal Hamburger Stand. It's at places like this that Elvis could blend in with the crowd and be just another good ol' American guy enjoying his good ol' American burger fresh off the grill. That's probably precisely why the King is now spotted at joints like Bob's in Hoboken. See if you can find him, and pass the mustard, please.

Elvis is alive, and still loves cheeseburgers, witnesses say

HOBOKEN, N.J.—Elvis Presley was sighted late yesterday evening at a local restaurant, according to Madge Farmell, head waitress of Bob's Restaurant. "He's polite, a perfect gentleman," Farmell stated. "He said, 'Yes

For Elvis, the only way to go was in the lap of luxury in custom-designed, top-of-the-line, no-holds-barred cars. Because of his unbridled passion for fancy autos, the King of Rock-and-Roll was also known as the King of the Road. Elvis collected cars like some people collect matchbooks. His spending habits would kick into overdrive just about anytime he set foot in a car dealership. When it came to cars, Elvis was as generous as he was frivolous. He routinely purchased cars not only for himself, but for family members, friends, employees and even total strangers. The King's former secretary once revealed that in a single month, her boss had purchased 33 vehicles, a total of more than one per day. On a single day in 1975, he purchased 14 Eldorados from Southern Motors in Memphis. On another day in the early '70s, he bought out 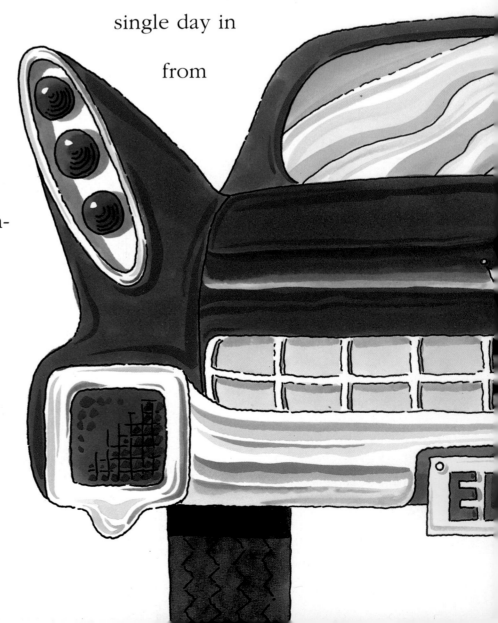 Schelling Lincoln-Mercury's entire stock of five Lincoln Continental Mark IVs. And at another time, he loaded up on 30 four-wheel-drive Ford Rancheros, supposedly so his ranch hands could deftly maneuver the dirt roads on his

163-acre ranch. Elvis was never one to deprive himself of anything, especially if it was motorized metal. In the early '70s Elvis eyed the customized Dodge van of Conway Twitty. He liked it; he 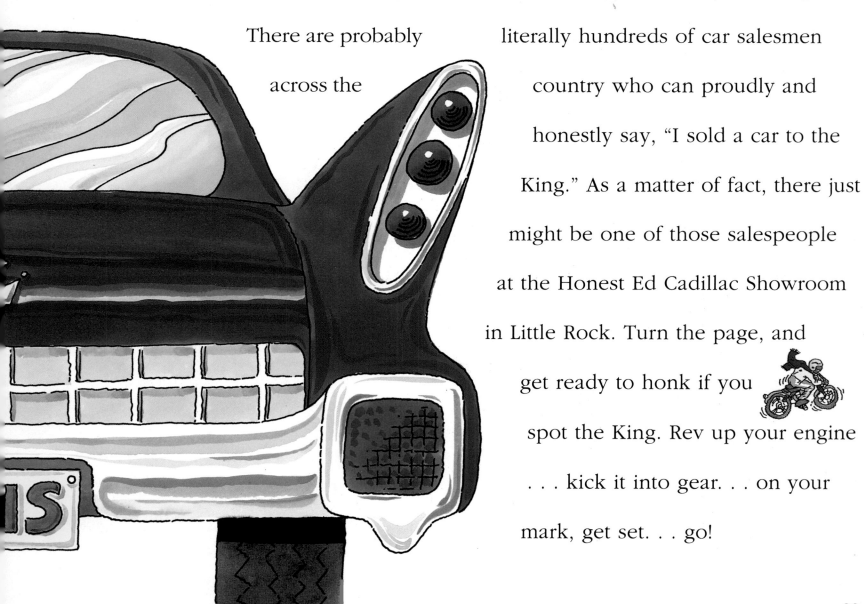 wanted one, so he got it. . . just picked up the phone, called Van Mann in Elkhart, Indiana, and ordered it like he was ordering a pizza: one customized van, brown with pictures of horses on the sides, a double bed, television set, air conditioning, refrigerator, burglar alarm, tape deck and hold the anchovies, please (you get the drift). Elvis was the proud owner of Harley Davidson choppers, supertrikes and even snowmobiles (all customized, usually by Supercycle in Memphis).

There are probably literally hundreds of car salesmen across the country who can proudly and honestly say, "I sold a car to the King." As a matter of fact, there just might be one of those salespeople at the Honest Ed Cadillac Showroom in Little Rock. Turn the page, and get ready to honk if you spot the King. Rev up your engine . . . kick it into gear. . . on your mark, get set. . . go!

For spotting the King in all ten locations, you've earned your Genuine All-Shook-Up Elvis Sighti
the Hot 100. There's a top ten for each setting, and every one is counted down and ready to g

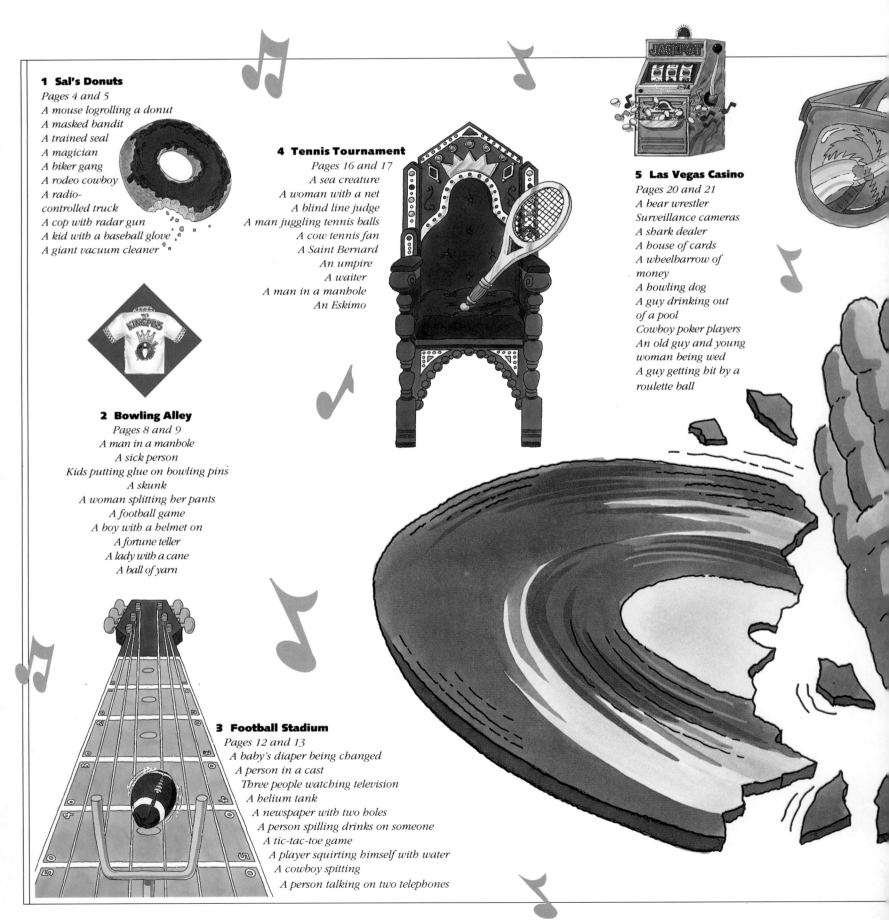

1 Sal's Donuts
Pages 4 and 5
A mouse logrolling a donut
A masked bandit
A trained seal
A magician
A biker gang
A rodeo cowboy
A radio-controlled truck
A cop with radar gun
A kid with a baseball glove
A giant vacuum cleaner

2 Bowling Alley
Pages 8 and 9
A man in a manhole
A sick person
Kids putting glue on bowling pins
A skunk
A woman splitting her pants
A football game
A boy with a helmet on
A fortune teller
A lady with a cane
A ball of yarn

3 Football Stadium
Pages 12 and 13
A baby's diaper being changed
A person in a cast
Three people watching television
A helium tank
A newspaper with two holes
A person spilling drinks on someone
A tic-tac-toe game
A player squirting himself with water
A cowboy spitting
A person talking on two telephones

4 Tennis Tournament
Pages 16 and 17
A sea creature
A woman with a net
A blind line judge
A man juggling tennis balls
A cow tennis fan
A Saint Bernard
An umpire
A waiter
A man in a manhole
An Eskimo

5 Las Vegas Casino
Pages 20 and 21
A bear wrestler
Surveillance cameras
A shark dealer
A house of cards
A wheelbarrow of money
A howling dog
A guy drinking out of a pool
Cowboy poker players
An old guy and young woman being wed
A guy getting hit by a roulette ball

ock-and-Roll Wings. You found the Big Number One, and now here's your chance to track down
t's shake, rattle and roll, all the way down this hit parade — the King would want it that way!

6 Aloha Again
Pages 24 and 25
A shark fin surfacing on the beach
A grass skirt on fire
Angry cows
A sea creature
A body surfer
A sheriff riding a seahorse
A snow skier
A vampire
An ostrich with its head buried
A knight

8 WackoWorld
Pages 32 and 33
A monkey in a tree
A stuffed beaver
Ducks shooting at people
A bald lady
A woodpecker
A long-haired dog
Kids on leashes
A pirate
A man playing horns
An aerial dogfight

9 Bob's Restaurant
Pages 36 and 37
A mouse stealing cheese
Girls playing jacks
A man in a gas mask
Busboys playing cards
A grass skirt on fire
An alligator
Boys tripping a waitress
A sleeping bat
Boys tossing a football
A large roach

10 Honest Ed Cadillac
Pages 40 and 41
An alligator
A mermaid
A sleeping vampire bat
A lovesick cow
Sardines
Escaped convicts
A bar of soap
A shark
A sea creature
A caveman

7 Karate Match
Pages 28 and 29
A man painting belts
Someone kicking out of a bag
A knight in shining armor
A knife juggler
A man slicing pizza with his hand
A grasshopper
A bald man with four belts
A man with a belt for a hat
A rabbit eating a carrot
A balding man with four belts

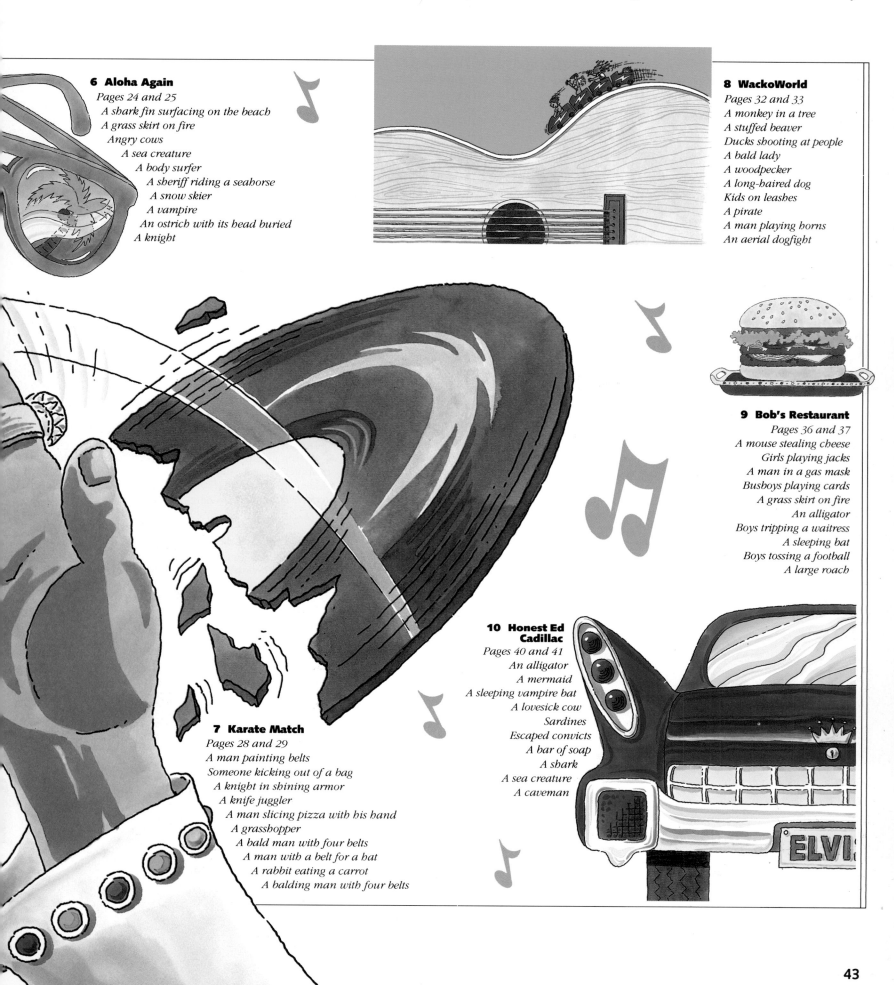

Q When and where was Elvis born?
A Elvis was born Elvis Aron Presley on January 8, 1935, at 306 Elvis Presley Drive (formerly Old Saltillo Road) in East Tupelo, Mississippi.

Q Was Elvis an only child?
A Elvis had a twin brother, Jesse Garon, who died at birth.

Q Where was Elvis' first public performance, and what did he sing?
A In 1945, a 10-year-old Elvis won second prize at his first public performance – a talent contest at the annual Mississippi-Alabama Fair and Dairy Show. He sang "Old Shep," a tear-jerker about a boy who has to put his dog to sleep. Eleven years later, Elvis returned to Tupelo to perform at the same show on a day declared "Elvis Presley Day" by the state.

Q When did Elvis get his first guitar?
A His mother Gladys bought Elvis his first guitar from Tupelo Hardware in January 1946. Young Elvis really wanted a .22 rifle, but Gladys feared it was too dangerous and picked the guitar instead.

Q What was Elvis' first record?
A April 1953 – Elvis cut his first record, "My Happiness", as a birthday gift for his mother Gladys. It was recorded in Sun Studio (called the Memphis Recording Service at that time) and was home to Sun Records.

Q What was Elvis' high school alma mater?
A Elvis graduated from L.C. Humes High School in Memphis in the summer of 1953.

Q Why was Elvis bullied in high school?
A Elvis was often bullied when he was in high school because he had long, greasy hair.

Q What was Elvis' first job?
A Elvis' first job was as a cinema usher at Loew's State Cinema. He was soon fired for punching another usher.

Q What were some of his other jobs?
A Elvis worked the late shift at Marl Metal Products while still in high school but had to quit because he was falling asleep during his classes. In July 1953, 18-year-old Elvis took his first full-time job at the Precision Tool Company, then left that fall to work as a truck driver for the Crown Electric Company. In November 1954, Elvis left his job at Crown Electric to go on the road.

Q What is significant about July, 1954?
A Elvis, Scotty Moore and Bill Black recorded "That's All Right (Mama)", his first hit song, released by Sun on July 5. On July 30, he made his debut as a public performer at The Shell in Overton Park.

Q True or False: Elvis' Grand Ole Opry appearance was one of the biggest successes of Elvis' early career.
A False: On September 25, 1954, Elvis performed on radio's Grand Ole Opry, but his style and performance didn't go over well with the conservative crowd, and the Opry's manager and booking agent told him to go back to driving a truck.

Q What was Elvis' self-styled nickname?
A When Elvis began to perform in the Memphis area after the release of his first record on the Sun label in August 1954, he sometimes called himself the Hillbilly Cat. It wasn't long before his own name was better known.

Q What was his first major tour?
A In May of 1955, Elvis and the Blue Moon Boys started their first major tour as part of Hank Snow's All-Star Jamboree. When the crowd saw Elvis in Jacksonville, Florida, a riot started.

Q What was Elvis' first number one record?
A Elvis got his first number one record in November 1955 when "Mystery Train" shot up to number one on the Country Charts. Soon after, in January 1956, Elvis recorded other popular hits: "Heartbreak Hotel", "Blue Suede Shoes", "Tutti Frutti" and "Shake, Rattle and Roll."

Q What was his first television appearance?
A On January 28, 1956, Elvis first appeared on the Tommy and Jimmy Dorsey "Stage Show."

Q When did Tom Parker become Elvis' manager?
A In March 1956, Colonel Tom Parker took over as Elvis' manager and "Heartbreak Hotel" reached number one on the country and western and R & B charts.

Q What was Elvis' first motion picture?
A *Love Me Tender* was Elvis' first motion picture, and grossed six times what it cost. It was the only film in which Elvis "died," and because many fans were outraged and genuinely distressed when they saw Elvis dying on the screen, Hollywood decided that he would never again die in a part.

Q With what motion picture company did he have a contract?
A In April 1956, Elvis flew to Hollywood to make a screen test for Paramount Pictures, resulting in a seven-year contract for three films. He went on to make a total of 33 films.

Q What was another nickname for Elvis, this time not his own?
A A derogatory nickname for Elvis Presley, invented in Hollywood, was "Elvis Pretzel." Some say the name was given him by Humphrey Bogart.

Q What were some of Elvis' pastimes?
A Two of his favorite activities were roller skating and going to the cinema, and he used to have to hire a cinema or a skating rink in the early hours of the morning to avoid the crowds that flocked to him. Elvis also organized his own football team, the Elvis Presley Enterprisers, to play against other stars' teams on Sundays at DeNeve Park in Bel Air.

Q What was Elvis' biggest hit of the 50s'?
A In July 1956 Elvis recorded "Hound Dog", his biggest hit single of the 1950s.

Q What hit song did he record while standing in a stairwell?
A In 1956 Elvis recorded "Heartbreak Hotel" while standing in a stairwell, to produce its haunted, echoing sound.

Q What toothpaste did he use?
A Elvis always brushed with Colgate toothpaste.

Q What was his favorite cologne?
A Elvis's favorite cologne was Brut, by Fabergé.

Q What size clothing did he wear?
A Size 16-35 shirt and size 11D shoe fit Elvis.

Q What television show host refused to have Elvis and later altered its decision?
A Ed Sullivan said he would never have Elvis on his show, but in 1956 signed Elvis to a $50,000 contract.

Q Where did he live before moving to Graceland?
A For a little over a year, before purchasing Graceland, Elvis lived at 1034 Audubon Drive in Memphis. At the age of 22, Elvis purchased Graceland and 13.8 acres of surrounding land for $102,500 from Dr. and Mrs. Thomas Moore, who named the home for Mrs. Moore's great aunt, Grace. Elvis lived there from 1957 to 1977. In 1972, the twelve-mile stretch of U.S. Highway 51 was renamed Elvis Presley Boulevard.

Q Did he own other properties?
A Elvis bought the 163-acre Circle G Ranch in Mississippi for $300,000 in February 1967 at the height of his interest in horses. Elvis later lost the wedding ring Priscilla gave him on the Circle G ranch.

Q Who was John Burrows?
A "John Burrows" was the code name Elvis gave to close friends so they would be able to get through to him at Graceland.

Q What was the Memphis Mafia?
A The so-called Memphis Mafia was a group of close buddies that constantly surrounded Elvis and kept him company, acting as gofers, bodyguards, playmates, and confidants for The King. Elvis Presley's entourage was given the nickname "El's Angels" in recognition of their generally rowdy behavior. Elvis sometimes referred to his entourage as "The Twelve," and they referred to him as the "Big E."

Q When was Elvis drafted into the army?
A Elvis received a draft notice on December 10, 1957, and was ordered to report to the Memphis draft board on January 10, 1958 – a date which conflicted with the filming of his fourth movie, *King Creole*. Elvis applied for and was granted a postponement until March 25, 1958.

Q What was the public's reaction to Elvis' being drafted?

A Elvis' fans organized a country-wide petition demanding that Elvis be designated a "national treasure" to prevent his being drafted in 1957. Elvis himself rented the Rainbow Skating Rink for eight consecutive nights of skating parties before he went into the army. In March 1958, he was sent to Fort Hood, near Killeen, Texas for his basic training. On January 20, 1960, Elvis was promoted to sergeant. On March 5, 1960 he was discharged.

Q What was Elvis' first gold record?

A Presley received his first gold record on August 11, 1958, to mark the fact that his single "Hard Headed Woman" had sold one million copies. Shortly after this distinction, RCA submitted many of his earlier hits for gold certification.

Q When did Elvis meet Priscilla?

A Priscilla Beaulieu was 14 years old when Elvis first met and fell in love with her in September 1959. When Priscilla graduated from high school in the summer of 1963, Elvis gave her a bright red Corvair as a graduation present.

Q Did Elvis ever meet the Beatles?

A In August 1965, Elvis met the Beatles at his house in Perugia Way, Beverly Hills. Under Elvis' orders, no photos or recordings were allowed. The Beatles were awestruck to be in the presence of the King.

Q Who did Elvis say was the best singer in the world?

A Elvis once called Roy Orbison the best singer in the world.

Q Did he have a pet?

A Among his many dogs, including a pet collie named Baba, Elvis had a chow named Getlo, of which he was especially fond.

Q What were Elvis' favorite foods?

A In addition to donuts, cheeseburgers and home-cooking of all kinds, but especially fried chicken, Elvis liked to snack on grilled peanut-butter-and- banana sandwiches. He even flew the *Lisa Marie* to Denver for some.

Q What was Elvis' most extravagant automobile?

A In the mid-1960s, Elvis ordered a custom Cadillac from Barris Kustom City of North Hollywood. It was almost a "solid gold Cadillac," with gold-plated bumpers and hubcaps.

Q When were Elvis and Priscilla married?

A On May 1, 1967 Elvis (32) and Priscilla (21) were married in Las Vegas.

Q What was Priscilla's nickname for Elvis?

A "Fire Eyes" was the nickname Priscilla Presley used for her husband when he was in an angry mood.

Q Did they have children?

A Lisa Marie Presley was born to Elvis and Priscilla at Baptist Memorial Hospital on Madison Avenue in Memphis on February 1, 1968. Elvis frequently called his daughter Lisa Marie "Yisa."

Q What were Elvis' mottos?

A All of Elvis' male employees were given gold necklaces bearing the TCB-and-lightning bolt emblem. It stood for Taking Care of Business in a Flash, Elvis' motto. For the women in Elvis' life, there were gold necklaces with the TLC emblem. It stood for Tender Loving Care, another motto of Elvis'.

Q What was "The Comeback"?

A On December 3, 1968 Elvis appeared on an NBC television special which became known as "The Comeback." The historic special marked his first live performance in almost eight years, a period during which he cranked out movies in Hollywood. Rock critic Griel Marcus wrote that this rough-and-tumble special contained the best music of Elvis' life: "If there was ever music that bleeds, this was it."

Q Did Elvis ever meet the President?

A The first president Elvis Presley met was Lyndon B. Johnson. LBJ stopped by the location shooting of *Spinout* in 1969. In December 1970, he met then-President Richard Nixon after hopping a commercial flight, alone, to Washington D.C. He passed a note to a White House guard and soon gained admittance.

Q Was he afraid of flying?

A For many years Elvis was afraid of flying. His fear was completely rational, in view of the fact that so many entertainers had been killed in crashes of small planes as they headed from one concert date to another. When he did get over this fear of flying, he did it in style; he bought an airplane and turned it into a "penthouse in the sky," naming it the *Lisa Marie*.

Q What was his attitude toward law enforcement?

A Elvis Presley collected badges from police departments and sheriff's offices all over the country. Nothing made him happier than membership in some law-enforcement body.

Q What piece of classical music was used by Elvis?

A Elvis always used the symphonic piece "Also Sprach Zarathustra," by Richard Strauss to open his live shows in the last decade of his performing career. The music is instantly recognizable as the theme from the movie *2001: A Space Odyssey*.

Q What were some of his awards?

A In January 1971, Elvis was named one of the ten "Outstanding Young Men of the Year" by the American Junior Chambers of Commerce. In August of that same year Elvis was given the Bing Crosby Award by the National Academy of Recording Arts and Sciences. He received three Grammy awards, each for a gospel song: "How Great Thou Art" in 1967; "He Touched Me" in 1972, and "How Great Thou Art" (remake) in 1974.

Q What was his last film?

A Elvis started work on his last film, *Elvis On Tour*, a revealing look at the star at work and at play, both on-stage and off, in March 1972.

Q Did Elvis ever appear at Madison Square Garden in New York?

A Yes, in August 1972.

Q What was the first internationally broadcast television show?

A *Aloha From Hawaii* with Elvis Presley, in 1973, was the first show ever to be broadcast by satellite throughout the world.

Q Why is his middle name spelled two ways?

A Elvis Presley's birth certificate spells his middle name "Aron," whereas on his tombstone it is spelled "Aaron." His father, Vernon, misspelled his son's middle name on the birth certificate. Later, Elvis had his middle name legally changed to the conventional spelling.

Q What tributes to Elvis were there, after his death?

A In late 1977 after Elvis' death on August 16, a musical based on his life was staged in London and won an award for best musical production. In 1978, a tribute to him appeared in the form of a Broadway show, *Elvis Lives*. In Memphis, the Elvis Presley Trauma Center has been established and is supported by donations from Elvis fans all over the world. The city of Memphis also erected a larger-than-life statue of its most famous citizen on a small area of grass on downtown Beale Street, renamed Elvis Presley Plaza.

And on May 18, 1979, the Elvis Presley Memorial Chapel was opened in East Tupelo, Mississippi.

Q Was there an international tribute?

A To commemorate the day, exactly thirty years earlier, that Elvis and his military unit had arrived, a life-size statue of Elvis was erected on October 1, 1988, on a dock in Bremerhaven, Germany.

Q How generous was Elvis?

A For most of his career, Elvis wrote more than $100,000 in checks every year to various charities he supported. He also gave family, friends and even complete strangers extravagant gifts.

Q What happened to Elvis' parents?

A His mother, Gladys, died of a heart attack in August 1958. In July 1979, Elvis' father, Vernon, died of heart failure.

Q When did Graceland open for public tours?

A Graceland opened to the public in June 1982. Every year at Graceland, the week immediately preceding the day Elvis died, August 16, 1977, is celebrated as International Tribute Week. Graceland becomes Lisa Marie's on February 1, 1993 – her 25th birthday.